I0115834

She's So Bipolar

Veronica Cronin

Copyright © 2013 Veronica Cronin

All rights reserved.

ISBN: 0615813763
ISBN-13: 9780615813769

DEDICATION

For Kristina, Kevin, and Lou

INTRODUCTION

A red towel, a razor blade, and the coolness of the

tub were under me. I am nude, and there is no

water in the tub. No, that isn't the purpose. The

intent is clear: kill myself and leave as little mess as

possible. Well, I didn't say it was a good idea. I

didn't say it was sane. However, I can report that at

that very moment, with tears streaming down my

face and my husband jiggling the door, I wanted to

die.

I couldn't think of a single reason to live. I had

calmly walked into the bathroom, locked the door,

dropped my clothes, and got into the tub. I

thought, red towel for red blood. Why was I

thinking these thoughts? I had a history of

depression, and I idealized suicide before, but I never thought I would get to this point. I had just graduated from the community college, was a mother of a seven-year- old, and wife to a great guy. I was happy. I wanted to die. Would I?

As I sat there, oblivious to my husband trying to get into the door, I turned my hands over and looked at my veins and arteries below my skin. Would it hurt? Of course it would. I scratched at my skin with the antique razor blade from a family shaving set. *Something old.*

Ow! This is when I remembered that men usually go out in a dangerous way. Women go as quietly as possible: pills or poison. Why didn't I do that?

I could hear my husband at the door, using a

screwdriver this time.

All I could think of was the pain, the pain my body felt as I sat there, shivering. My tears would go away. Whatever was putting these thoughts in my head would be squashed. I had to get through the blood first. That was a problem.

My husband came into the room. Shit. Well, he had to get me out of this tub first.

"Don't come near me," I said.

He replied, with an outstretched hand, "You want Kristina to find you this way?"

Why did he have to use her? As he took away the blade and towel, he helped lift me out of the tub and tucked me into bed. I caught a glimpse of myself in the mirror: hair mussed, tear-streaked face, and very dark circles under my eyes. Would I ever look like myself again? Where did that happy girl go?

I slipped under the cool sheets, and took one of the doctor's magic pills to help me sleep and calm me down. I had survived. Whoopee. Hubby put on David Letterman, and I tried to laugh. It did lull me to sleep. Television always lulls me, because I don't feel alone.

What I dreaded the most was the daylight

Contents

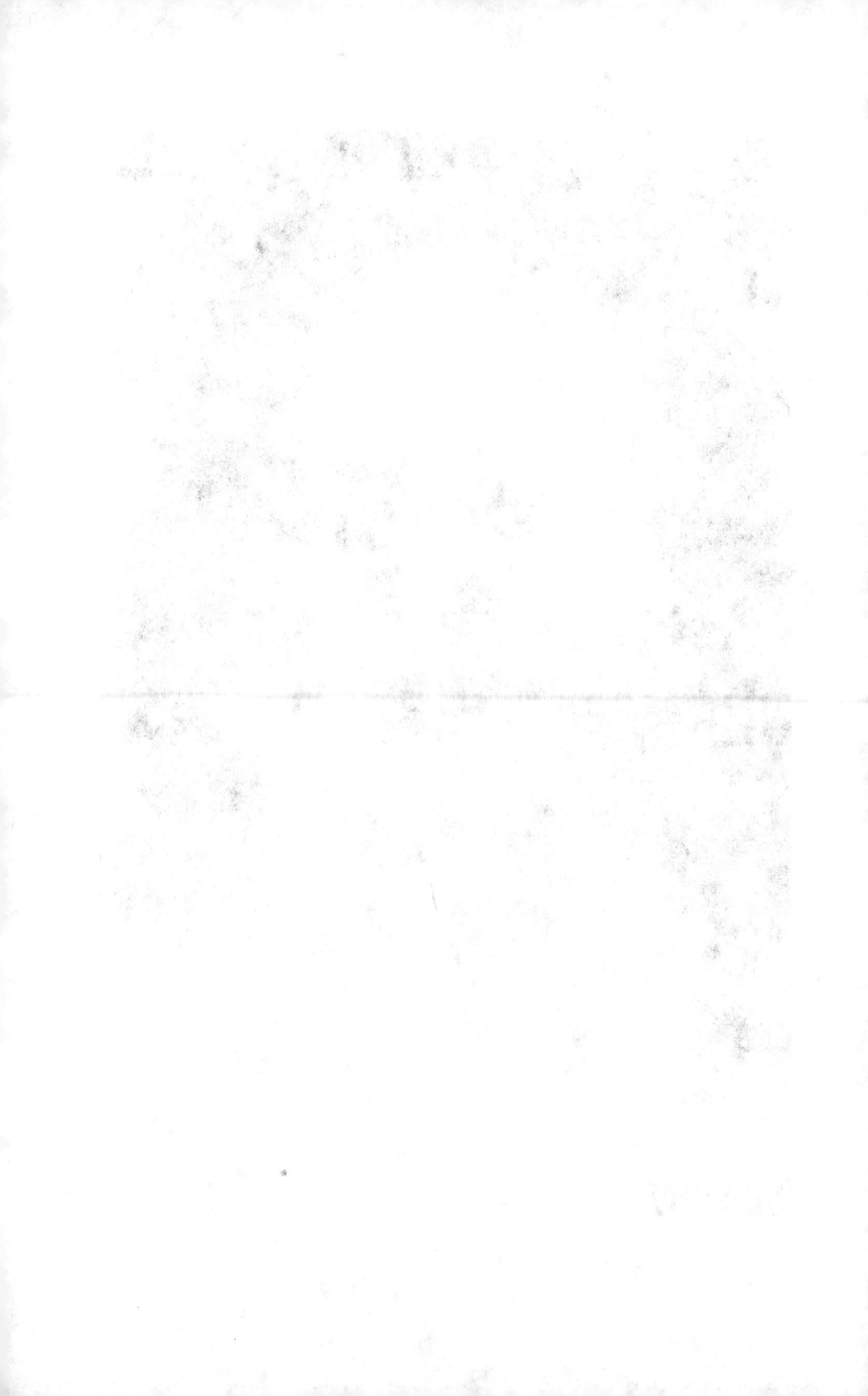

WHY WRITE ABOUT BIPOLAR ILLNESS?

"Oh, she's sooo bipolar!" Ever heard that? That's just one reason to write about the truth of living with the disease.

No one knows exactly what it is.

We use it to describe anyone that's odd, different, or downright loony. Which, of course, we assign to being eccentric, but the terms loony, crazy, mad, etc., can be a bit insulting. The general public uses the illness to describe non-bipolar people all the time, but they don't realize what they are saying. Truly.

In the '80s, we called people "schizo." It's done with many illnesses of the mind. It shouldn't be talked about so casually with so many falsehoods.

That's why I chose to write this book. Besides, it's a form of therapy that's free! I'll tell you about what being Bipolar I with rapid cycling and seasonal disorder is like: the mania, depression, and the panic attacks.

I'll tell you how family, friends, and co-workers have handled me, what it's like to be a mom with bipolar - an inheritable illness, and day -to-day struggles and triumphs. Oh yeah, you didn't know there are triumphs? There are. And I plan to have many more.

DESPAIR

2
HOW I WAS DIAGNOSED

Disclaimer: Any and all treatment that I talk about is for me and me alone, everyone is different, and you should seek your own treatment if you suspect you are or you are Bipolar.

1997: I had just graduated from Palm Beach Community College, when I entered Florida Atlantic University and began having symptoms, but I didn't know they were symptoms for a few months. I wasn't sure what was happening to me. I graduated with honors at 30, and I was happier than I'd ever been - that's good stress. It began with lethargy and sleep. I was exhausted constantly. My daughter was seven at the time, and didn't quite understand why we would have a nap every day after school.

Vertigo hit me next, as I was constantly dizzy. I was

flat in emotions. By Christmas, I was so lethargic

that I had to be pushed around Disney in a

wheelchair. I still had no idea what was happening.

Just before the Disney trip, I began to seek

treatment. Since I was a military spouse, I was seen

at the VA Hospital in West Palm Beach, FL. They

were excellent. They had me see my primary, of

course, then on to the neurologist. He gave me a CT

Scan and an MRI (where I found out that I go into

shock when given iodine dye and am claustrophobic

... good times.), and found nothing. He suspected a

tumor or Multiple Sclerosis. I had neither. Since I

had developed a tingling in my face - which to today

no one can explain to me, I was sent to the

neurologist. Since he couldn't find one physical

thing wrong with me, he sent me on to the psychiatric department.

The first doctor I saw put me on an anti-depressant called Zoloft.

By February, I was manic.

In many bipolar patients, an anti-depressant alone can cause mania, and I was diagnosed in this way. After a lengthy history was taken, many signals went off to them: an abusive childhood, manic and depressed as a teen, I was 30, a prime age for diagnosis, a writer, as creative types are prone, and a family history of depression.

With the physical symptoms of mania clearly present: insomnia, spending money, rapid speech, hard to focus, and suicidal, I was a shoe-in to be medicated and treated as a Bipolar patient. They put me on a cocktail of Carbemazepine, Klonopin, Prozac, and Risperdal.

And I slept over 12 hours a day for 18 months before I got leveled off. It sucked. BUT, it wasn't a tumor. I had to be grateful.

After a crying jag.

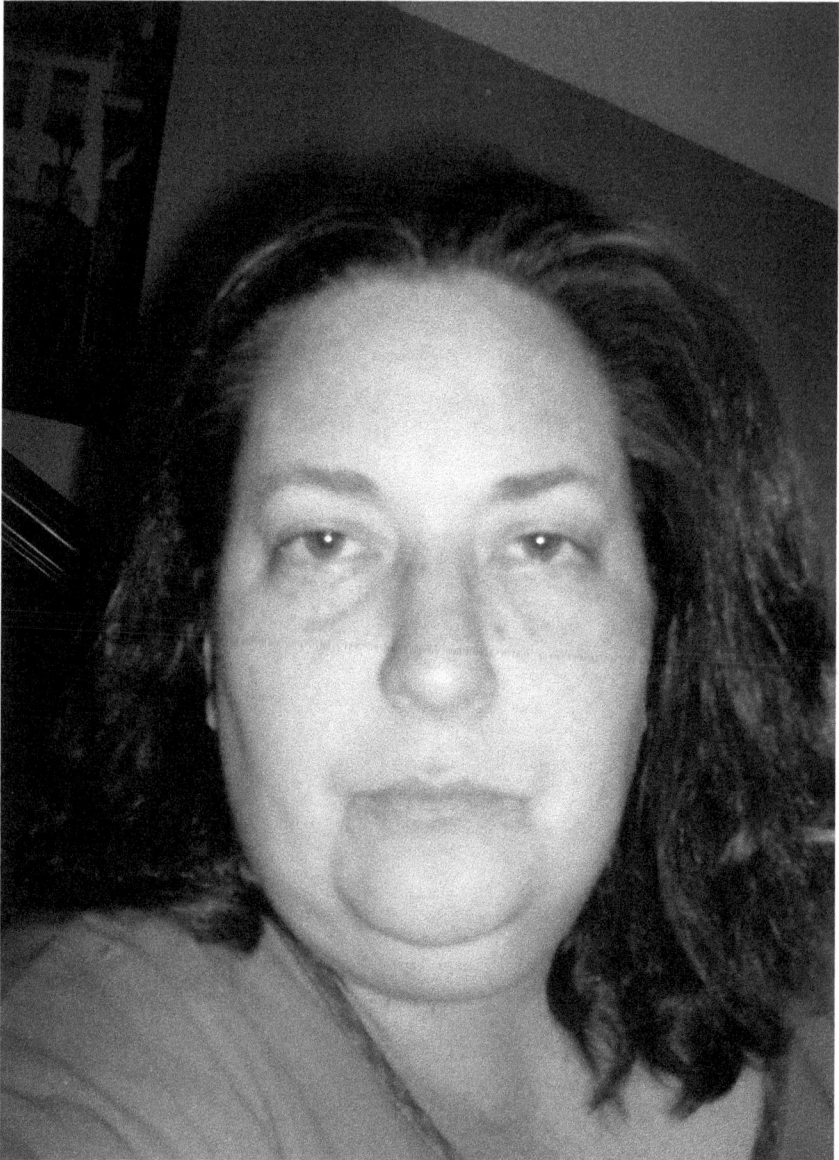

Telling Your Children

When your mother looks like the pictures in this book, it's hard to explain it to your children, or child, in my case. Kristina was only seven when I was diagnosed, and I suppose I seemed like a mostly fun mom till the first deep depression at age 30. Why? I ride high, mostly hypomanic to manic, and I was always full of adventure and doing things with her.

Until that day.

I had already been checked out for a brain tumor and MS, and she went through all of the testing with me. That was scary enough for her, but it was the one thing I said while crying one day that she'll never forget: "God has left me."

Years later, she told me she knew something was wrong then, as I had never said anything like that before and it was shocking to her.

You have to be careful with how you tell them. Not because of their age - they live with you, after all, and they know and watch you more than you think.

When I told Kristina, I said that "My brain has a sickness, like a cold, except it won't go away, and I'll have to take medicine now.

She understood this, and we had long talks about it when issues or emotional overrides of meds happened. Later, it was the full weight of the illness that I told her about, and the fact that it's hereditary.

That little tidbit was hard. I would never wish this illness on anyone, yet I could possibly pass it on to her.

She's in her twenties now, and she knows me better than most anyone. I suppose when your parent is ill, you observe even more. She certainly has gone through some tough times with me, and I'm not the easiest person to live with. Constant anxiety, mood shifts, and paranoia about people's intentions are hard to explain to a young person, but you have to.

They see it everyday, so they must know *what to do* in an emergency. It's better to be honest about bad situations than hide them away.

She knows now that I need her. I've stayed alive for her. That's a heavy burden, I know, but the thought of her gets me through the deepest of depressions and the rages of mania. As long as someone remembers to mention her, I'm fine. But then, she's okay when she thinks of me. You can still be a strong parent with the illness.

Your children will respect you for it and work harder to understand you. That's the best payoff. Why? Not many people understand Bipolar illness, so when your child does, it's like a gift, from heaven.

Angry and getting manic …

4

Relationships and Marriage

Being bipolar is hard enough when you're alone, much less bringing someone else into the mix. We bipolar patients get sick of ourselves sometimes, and I feel like it's unfair to subject someone else to the ugly part of the disease. Hell, even the "good" parts of it are hard to take at times.

It's difficult to explain the constant monitoring that needs to take place, but my husband and daughter say that if you love someone, then it doesn't matter. I think it does. I'm pretty sure the disease and my handling of it contributed to my divorce years ago. I've become more efficient in handling myself, so there are tools that I use to "beat the system" of the illness.

1. Be completely and totally honest. If you aren't, no one can or will want to help you. It's hard when your impulse is to spend money and behave recklessly in mania, or when you're down deep in depression, but that's when you need people the most. They can't trust you if you aren't honest.

2. Laugh. A lot. If you can't laugh at this twist of fate, then you aren't going to get anywhere. Some things may not be funny at the time, but they will be later on, and at some point, you must laugh at it all. If you are having trouble, then watch a funny movie or a comedian. It works.

3. Tell your significant other when you are having suicidal thoughts. It is most crucial to do this, as

they know best how to bring you out of it, and if they can't, then they can take you to get the help you need. Don't dismiss any type of gloom and doom talk. You just never know when someone can be serious. For example: I may just need to talk, not a full-blown intervention, but you don't know that unless you ask.

4. Have a plan ready for everything. Plan for trips, when the illness strikes hard, or a simple get-together with friends. Many things can throw you off balance, so you might as well have prepared a plan for it all. Use a code word to get out of a situation. If I mention our code word, my man knows that I need to leave wherever we are due to overstimulation, tiredness, or even just needing to decompress and take my meds.

We may be at a party or family function, and I can get buggy and impatient. It means I need to take a med, get out of a situation with people, and just relax. It's hard hiding your real emotions when your brain is saying go for it. It's exhausting, really.

5. "Legalize yourself." Get all the documents you need signed by both of you if he/she is the one to care for you. Sign health directives, wills, health surrogate paperwork, and have a list of doctors and your hospital at your fingertips. Pick up a few extra of your doctor's business cards and give them to people you are with a lot and you trust. They can take it from there.

If you try to be flexible and are trying these suggestions, then things will run more smoothly. I didn't do that the first time around. I should have, but I didn't know how important they really are. It took my present husband to read all he could about the disease and teach me. Good thing I'm a willing student...

WAITING FOR MY LOVE…

5

Bipolar: Your Family and Friends

Ever feel like your family and friends don't understand you, never have, and are potentially afraid of you? They don't and they are. It's called stigma. No single person can fully understand what someone else goes through if they do not go through it themselves.

It's impossible.

I don't know what it's like to not have this illness, and I can't comprehend how so many things that I freak about have no meaning to most. So, how could anyone possibly know what it feels like to be me? I have to constantly be aware of that.

I had a friend tell me today that she understood the illness better through my writings, but that she doesn't know what to do to help. Well, that's the first thing she could do: show interest and ask. So many people don't even want to bring it up to the "affected person," because they are leery of the reaction they could get.

I admired my friend for asking, (she's a smart cookie) and we simply chatted by private message on Facebook. It lifted me, and being a writer herself, she got me right back on to thinking about writing. My mood lifted, and I didn't feel alone.

When I was first diagnosed, I lost a few friends. They didn't know how to handle it or were afraid. As long as I'm on my meds, just like any other illness, I'm mostly even. Now, the brain has a tendency to wreak havoc by overriding meds sometimes, but I just wade through the muck until it clears.

I also gained a few friends - better ones, which were like me in some way, either a depressive or a bipolar patient, and creative. It's such a relief to be around people like me - and there are a lot more of us than you think.

Telling family was very hard, and still today, some do not understand it or even have compassion. I've been told a myriad of things, but the main point is very clear: not many understand this illness and think we are all nut jobs. This is evident immediately upon diagnoses. "Well that explains a lot," and more are common comments, and they did hurt. I've grown immune to them - because if they want to understand, they'd come stay for a week. Ha!

At the same time, I have family and friends that I know I could knock on their door in the middle of the night and I'd be let in. My grandmother always used that as a barometer for a good friend, and it's true. There are those I count on immensely to help me watch for mood shifts and the like. They accept me as I am, and truly, that's all you need to do as a family member: accept them.

We accept a lot of shit in our families: alcoholism, abuse, disrespect, children coming back home later in life, and a myriad of emergent situations... and that's a sample. If we accept or have lived through any of that - then a mental illness is cake. Of course, maybe only half-baked. Ha... See? Even those of us that are ill make jokes. We do it to disarm the intensity of the situation, and it usually works, but you have to be pretty tight with a bipolar to make fun of their illness. It took me a long time to grow immune to the teasing - by anyone. Of course, you don't get teased if you don't tell anyone, but then - you would be constantly explaining unusual behavior.

One of the biggest problems I have and others have as well, is that if we are having a bad day, we cancel our plans. This is difficult on all of my relationships. We simply can't fathom going out of the door that day. Loads of people don't understand this, but it is agoraphobic-like. Not exactly where we can't ever leave the house, but the world seems so overwhelming that we can't deal with the overstimulation, traffic, noise, crowds, and feeling vulnerable. It's actually quite terrifying.

Luckily, I have a close circle of friends that understand, but I know it wears thin on them. Why? Because I detest it. Don't you think we'd rather be out having fun? I know I would.

The best thing I've found in handling friends and family is to simply be very direct and very honest. It saves hurt feelings, and if I explain how I'm feeling, usually we can make alternate plans. Being direct is important. There is so much misinformation out there, which you really have to keep it simple. It's hard enough for us to understand it!

A night without sleep ... very common.

6

Medication Cocktails

After I was put on the med cocktail in 1998, it took 18 months to balance me out. I was a zombie. I hated it. I detested the way I felt: lethargic, forgetful, and non-productive. However, it was better than the symptoms of the illness. The hardest thing I had to adjust to was feeling "normal."

I had either been low in depression or high on mania my whole life. It really exhibited itself in my teens, but teens are very difficult to diagnose, because a lot of the symptoms are things that teens go through normally. I stayed on those meds for fourteen years. I think that's long, too. I'm glad you agree.

I just had a huge overhaul in late 2011. I went off the four meds I had been on all those years, and started three new ones: Abilify, Lamictal, Lunesta, and Klonopin. The Abilify works extremely well for me, the Lamictal has settled in well, and I was already on the Klonopin. You would think that it's enough to knock over a horse, but it doesn't affect me that way. I have a high tolerance.

I was unprepared for the withdrawal of the old meds. It was very physical and painful. I went into mania, and then I started see-sawing between the extremes for a month before I leveled off. I can't stand med changes. The docs tried to change my meds twice over the years, and they met resistance in my system. One med, Topamax, made my hair start to fall out. I lost a lot!

Most Bipolar patients have to be on a cocktail of meds. Not just one works, because of the variety of symptoms. There are a lucky few that only have to take lithium. That's uncommon. The cocktail of meds includes agents for sleep, anxiety, mood stabilization, anti-psychotics, and more. No one pill can do it all.

There are millions of bipolar people. You know one even if you don't know that they live with the illness. I'd bet my life on that one. We aren't all off meds like Charlie Sheen, as we take ours, work, and raise families like everyone else. It's just harder sometimes.

Me in the morning.

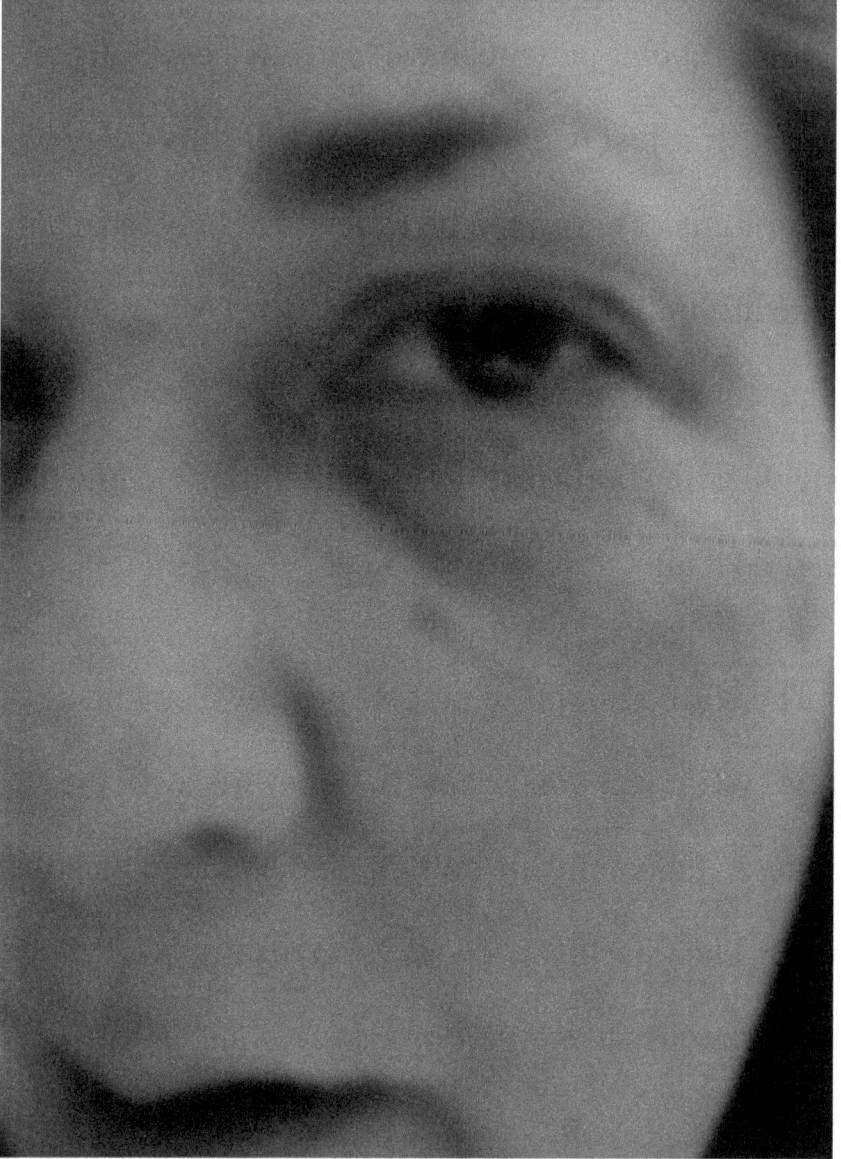

6

Mornings Are Hell

Morning is the absolute worst time of the day. The meds from the night before are still in my system, making me lethargic, and the minute I realize it's a new day? Panic attack. I have at least one mild to severe attack per day, usually in the morning.

Once my morning meds are in, I eat a little, and I rest for about half an hour - I feel better. Sometimes the panic and the fear overtake me for the morning, or perhaps the whole day. It comes out of nowhere, and my doctor says that I have triggers for them and that some simply do come out of nowhere.

I use several things to overcome them: light

therapy, music therapy, and walking or doing chores. If I sit in the sun for at least 10 minutes, I feel a lift in my mood and lethargy. I listen to music everyday, unless my ears are too sensitive to noise from a depression. I walk or complete chores to feel accomplished and keep my mind off of the pain. It eases around noon - two.

This morning is a good one, particularly because I'm writing. If I can get words out in a coherent manner, then I'm doing better than most days.

Since I have Bipolar I, which includes both depression and mania, rapid cycling, which means my mood constantly fluctuates (my husband says that if you don't like my mood - wait ten minutes.), and the seasonal component, which means I'm more depressed in the fall and more up in the spring, it

makes it all the more difficult to manage.   But - I

do. I have for 15 years diagnosed, and for 30 years

undiagnosed.   It is survivable. :)

A happy moment. I cherish them!

7

Panic Attacks

With panic attacks being featured in the previous chapter, someone asked me what they feel like. Not just the facts, which you can access through the NAMI - National Alliance on Mental Illness, but the feeling. I get why I was asked: it's because the normals, people without the illness, think that it's all in our minds, what is there to fear, and you're just trying to get attention. I understand that, because I never would have believed what it actually feels like: like I'm going to die.

It's a terrible feeling to wake up and not just dread the day, but panic over sunlight! As soon as I'm aware that it's morning, I immediately feel panic over the day ahead. My heart races, my mouth gets dry, I feel a bit dizzy, and I shake - inside and out. Sometimes I cry, when frustrated that it doesn't subside, but usually I'm just scared. The fear is palpable. My skin feels the fear, so I know it's not "all in my head." It's just my head that sends the signals!

My doctor tells me that panic attacks happen on their own and by triggers of stress - good or bad. That's right, you can have one on a good day. I have medication to take in the morning and throughout the day for the attacks, but if I wake and it's a bad one, well, I'm lethargic from the meds the rest of the day. It's no picnic. I can do without them.

A quiet moment.

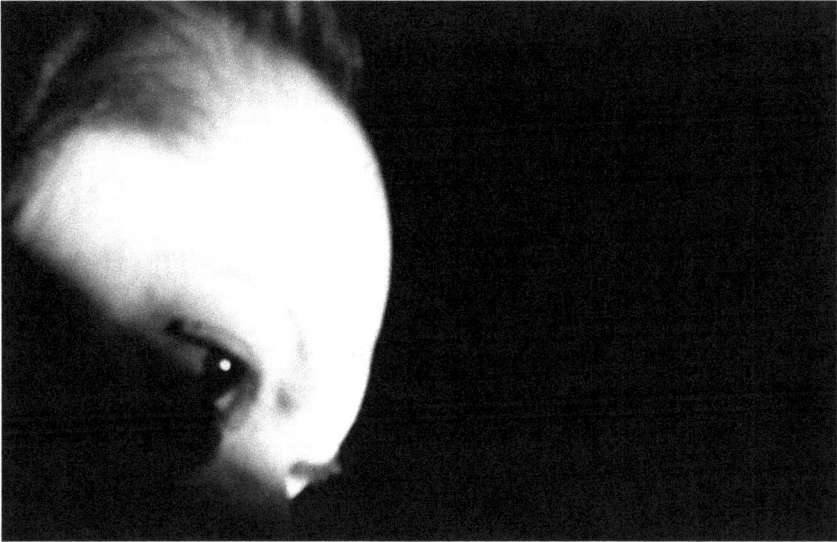

8

Hello Panic Attacks, Goodbye Day

Nothing pisses me off more than a panic attack out of nowhere. A major one was had this morning, and I still have the jitters... Upon waking, the day was a nightmare of fear, hyperventilating, and shaking. I don't know why it happened this morning, but it did. Some have a cause and some don't. The thing is, I had plans today: grocery shopping, tidying up, and I even had aspirations of baking. All for nothing.

The attack has paralyzed me for the day, and it is all I can do to remain calm. I'm not the C-word - Crazy. I'm just a normal person whose meds did not turn out to be enough today. Breakthroughs like this one are hard, because they are so unpredictable.

I feel like a total loser because so many people say, "Just think something else, get over it, go out and do something..." but they've no idea how terrifying going out of the door seems to be. It isn't that easy, and all the meds in the world can't take it all away. I have to ride it out. So, what do I do?

I immediately called my significant other to make him aware of the problem. This is not something to surprise someone with. I called my girlfriend, took a tranquilizer, and choked down some oatmeal. That all helped, but it's 2:30, and I'm still feeling jittery. I think I'll lay down with the dog now. She understands everything.

Animals are the best at calming me. Also kids and older people. Why? Animals have been shown to lower heart rates and make you live longer. Kids are fun to play with and you never know what they are going to say! They are so funny. Older people have great stories to tell. Love to sit and listen to all my older friends. They are too interesting. They are also patient, and understand my illness because of their life experiences.

Angry and depressed.

9

Depression: The Good, Bad, and The Ugly

When the dark moods hit me, transmitted by a faulty connection in my brain, I get pissed. Who wouldn't? Normal people have depression, but there are two kinds: situational and chemical. Situational can happen to anyone, including me.

Chemical is the type that you must be treated for regardless, and probably for life, because it's in your brain chemistry. For me, depression is one aspect of my illness, and it is one I can do without – at least in mania, I get things done!

I can go into a dark place very fast – due to rapid cycling, which means that I shift moods quickly, in a minute or an hour; I usually go through several moods a day. It's a bit exhausting. The depression saps everything from me. I feel like a wet noodle, as my grandmother would have said. There is no hope for a future, because it's hard to see one.

The symptoms are like that of a migraine: light sensitivity, headache, sensitivity to noise, irritability, and a lost feeling. Those are mine. There are many more – just check WebMD or the like.

Depression makes me lose faith: in myself, everyone, and even God. It's difficult to believe in things that seem meaningless in that moment. Suicidal thoughts are common in depression, and hell seems imminent, so what's the point of faith? I'm not attached to any one religion, but I have faith in a power larger than myself. It helps. The main reason that I have never been hospitalized or taken my life is because of my daughter. Whatever I've been through, it's all made better because of her. The thought of her takes me out of the dark corners of my mind and into some semblance of light.

Besides, both my parents are already gone. Since I know what that's like, I'd never intentionally do that to her. The hard part is telling my brain that little piece of info. Luckily, I have a great support system that reminds me.

I know many people who have either depression or are bipolar. There are many differences in the illnesses, but depression is depression, regardless of the diagnoses. Bipolar people are 25-50% more likely to commit suicide than the general

population, according to NAMI. People don't kill

themselves to hurt others or even to hurt

themselves. They do it, in my belief, to end the

pain. Many don't believe in psychic pain. No, not

psychic like someone giving you a reading, but the

mental and physical pain that your brain sets off in

a depression.

My skin hurts when I'm depressed.

I feel rushes of pain in my muscles and joints. My

mind is cloudy, my speech hard to handle – I have

trouble finding words. My face tingles constantly,

like Novocaine wearing off, and it is more noticeable

and sharp during an episode. These things are not

in my head. Many people think they are. Just like I

can't comprehend what it's like to have diabetes,

normal people can't imagine what it's like to be Bipolar. I get that. But don't ever disbelieve it. I assure you, it's real. And it sucks.

That's the bad and the ugly. What's good about depression? It's not mania.

Beyond Depair.

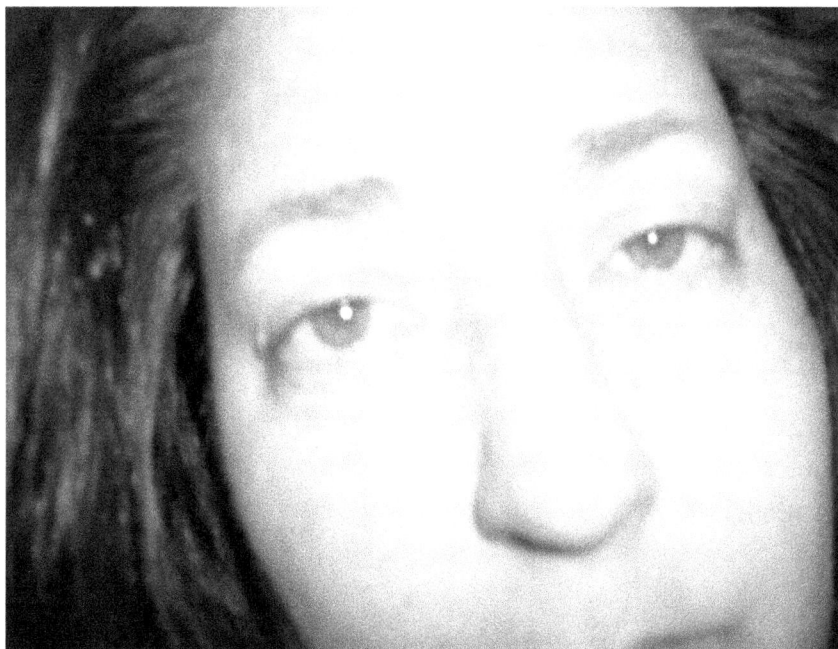

10

When Depression Hits Hard

My brain is funky sometimes. There are days that are awful. It's not the "normal blues," or just a sad day. Nothing situational is going on to set off the blues, and I get so lethargic that a shower is an effort. These are the times that people think you are faking or making excuses. Why? They can't see the illness.

Would you tell someone with a broken leg to "lighten up and walk already?" Would you tell them simply to "get over it?" No. When people can't see what's wrong with you, the sympathy card goes out the window. Not that we want sympathy. We actually crave empathy.

Mornings start out with a huge panic and anxiety attack, for seemingly no reason at all. This is the kind that I hate, because I've been doing so well, and I've been more stable than in a couple of months, that when it comes unexpectedly, it's even harder. It's like one day I am a prizefighter, and the next, I get knocked out.

These kinds of days make it hard to function normally. Normal is a silly little word, hated by those of us thought of as insane, but one word that we strive to be, if nothing else but to fit in. Funny though, the more I understand the illness, the more I realize that I am normal, just medicated.

My therapies don't work all the time, and that's hard. When the sunlight, a short walk, or some music doesn't work, then I have to just ride it out.

This is when I bring out the heavy hitters for lifting my mood: Kathy Griffin, Robin Williams, and other comedians, something yummy and comforting to eat (but not overdo), and snuggling. They don't cure depression, but they make it easier to bear.

One of my most trusted psychologists, for therapy, told me that some days you have to give in to your body to let it repair itself. I fought that for a long time, thinking it was just an excuse to be lazy. However, if I had gone to the dentist or had an out patient procedure, I'd rest for the day for the same reason. Rest is simply necessary. I suppose she was right – again.

Manic and angry at my husband for taking a picture of me, although I

pre-approved it.

11

Bipolar Mania

Mania is the exact opposite of being depressed, hence: bipolar. Spending sprees, racing thoughts, insomnia to the max, increased libido, feeling like I want to run a marathon, and other symptoms, such as: irritability, being snappy, argumentative, feeling like I'm queen of the world, knowing my "great ideas" will work, and an indestructible feeling are all part of my mania.

Everyone is different. Bipolar people all have unique brains, just like a thumbprint. That's why no two people are alike. No one med works for everyone. And no two people have the same symptoms.

I've never tried to hurt anyone else, and I've never felt like I would. I'm famous for slamming a door in a manic episode, but not people. Why should someone be physical hurt? They already have to deal with the episode, much less worry about being hit! It's not in my nature, anyway, and I don't add to the mania by drinking. That cuts out a lot of problems. Drinking makes me more hyper, so it increases the mania I already have.

I can see where many bipolar people get in trouble with the law – mixing the meds and alcohol, with an already fragile emotional state, well, it can bring down a person like a snap of the fingers. The illness is unpredictable with its moods, so reactions vary in any given situation.

Suicidal: Mania breeds pain ... of the mind and

the body. I've never wanted to die, really. My brain just thinks so. I want the pain to stop. Suicidal ideation, the thoughts of what you would do and how, are common in my mania. Thank goodness I tend to ride in hypomania, that hyper state that precedes mania, and can generally avoid most of the pain.

However, when it does come, I usually feel like getting a tattoo. Weird, right? Not after I figured it out: the act of tattooing redirects the psychic pain signals that are being sent out by my brain. My concentration switches to the new, "real" pain, and ends the other. It works. The problem is that I take more crap from people on my tats than anything else, so I only have six, all small but one.

What does it feel like? On the inside of my body, mania feels like my insides are on a super highway, going as fast as they can. What exactly would that be? My muscles are like the road and it feels like there is all this rushing on them.

The insomnia that is a byproduct of mania can actually make it worse. It always does with me, and that's why sleep is the number one priority for me. If I'm not sleeping, I won't be well. The less you sleep, the worse it gets, and then I start to feel like I'm going crazy, and I am – from sleep deprivation – and the mania. That's where meds come in, and they really knock you out. I also use music therapy for calming myself. This works wonders.

My frustration level is at an all-time high. Taking a picture of myself,

because I need to remember this, as it helps me manage my moods. It's

not pretty.

12

I'm Manic Now – An Experiment In Writing

Holidays always jack me up. I always wake early in the morning and can never go back to sleep. Like 4 a.m. I should say that I'm going to write this as it comes to me. My mind races a bit in mania or hypomania, and I'm in between both. I've not yet had my night meds, and I've not had enough sleep.

Getting sleep is essential to a stable person, and I've got a lot going on. I've got a wedding coming in June, moved recently, and have got the regular holiday "jumpies." Drama always surrounds holidays, as families and friends that don't normally see each other try to make a day of it. This day -

well, I didn't even make it to the family - the drama was on me this year!

My tire was in terrible shape, and with limited places open - Wal-Mart was, and we got a tire, but by the time we got it all done, we were already thirty minutes late and two hours away. My fiancé saved the day, and he took my daughter and me to lunch. Lovely, actually. We were the ones that didn't make it this year, and that's what I'm always afraid of. I suppose now that it has happened it should be no big deal.

Back to something important- I've been working on my wedding music lately, and was wondering if anyone has favorite eighties dance tunes. I bought a yoga mat, blocks, strap, and DVD this weekend, and

I can't wait to use it tomorrow. Not only friends, but also my psychiatrist has strongly urged me to practice yoga every day for not only exercise, but for meditation as well.

I've got cable again, and all that I've found on right now is Indiana Jones, the newest one, but I'd rather be watching David Tutera! I believe I'll wrap this I'll-regret-it-in-the-morning post, as I always feel I reveal too much, open myself up to much criticism, and I should just shut up already.

But the thing is, I think I have some piece of the human condition to share, and even in a rant - I can sound somewhat coherent. At least I could follow it. :) ...And you notice - I'm not doing something "crazy," or destructive, even though I won't sleep much tonight, even with meds, because I am so wound up. I'm actually being productive. And -

well, that's all that matters. No. If you're bipolar,

and reading this - you are not alone. You're not

crazy, either. It just feels like it sometimes.

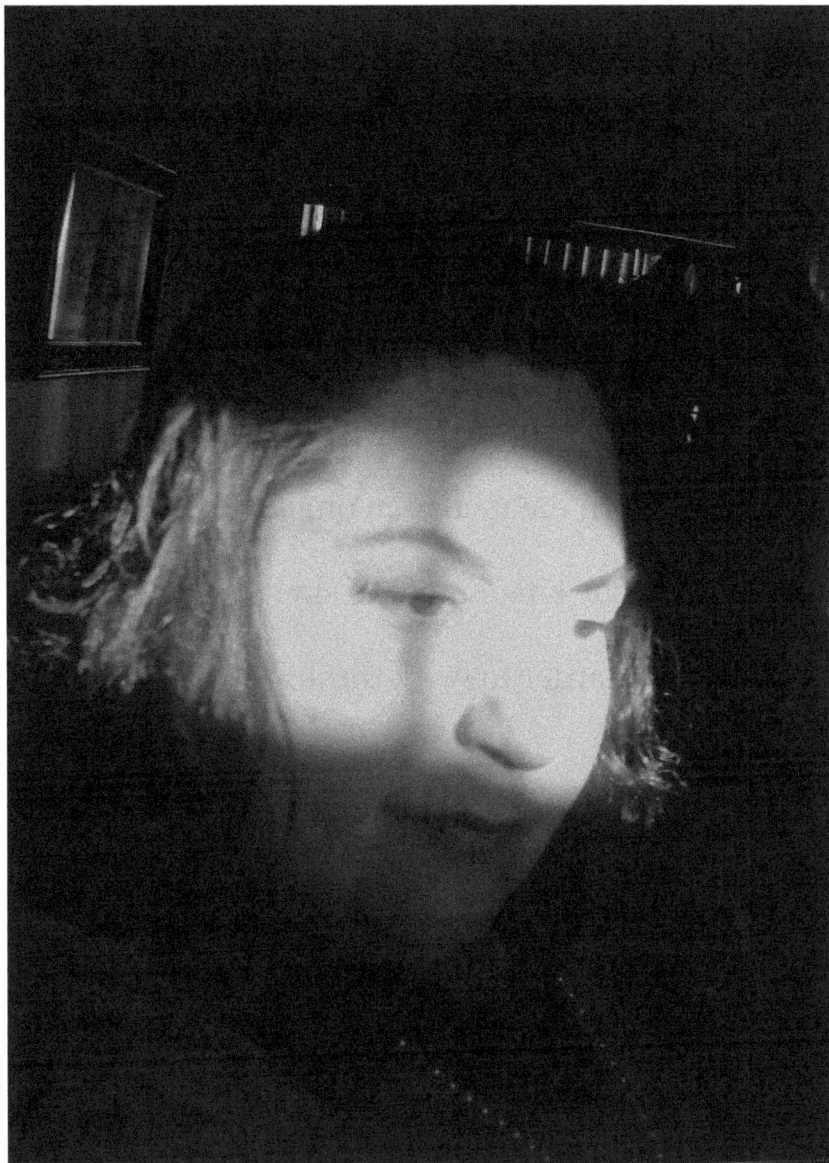

13

After Mania – The Crash

After mania, a crash comes. Similar to running or walking a marathon – your body hits a wall, and it goes limp. With the meds I'm on, it doesn't take long to bring the kite out of the sky. It's just limiting. It's harder to work through.

My mood, however, did not crash ... just that racing, manic feeling inside of me. I know I'll feel better in the late afternoon, after the meds have worn off, but it is frustrating to feel like I'm stuck in quicksand. I've got a slow mind and slow reactions.

When I have to go out or make an appointment, I'll wait till late afternoon. Usually, a trip to the grocery store when I'm like this, would feel like climbing a mountain, but, I try something that works: yoga. I've done it before. My doctor and others have been strongly suggesting yoga for physical exercise, but for meditation too, soothing the savage beast within.

I'll try that before going to the store, and perhaps I'll get a burst of that serotonin! It's got to be better than the lethargy.

14

Making Excuses

It's so incredibly easy to make excuses when you have an illness, particularly one with a depression component, which almost any would. When the depression hits hard or frequently during the day, it is tough. I don't want to do anything. I get panicky at all there is to do, and it is incredibly overwhelming.

And you don't see that you're making excuses for not getting up and doing things until you are in a rut. That's when you need your "caretaker" or a friend to help you push through it. You also need strength and guts of your own.

A friend of mine told me recently that I've got to

push harder. That seems a herculean task, considering the illness and meds that I take. I agree I need to get stronger and stop my excuses, so I simply did. I'm pushing through wanting to sleep, not eat, and not see friends.

I'm kind of sick of not living.

I was, and then a job change put me in an incredible funk. For three months. It reminds me of when my mother passed. I feel like I'm just standing still.

So, I got up. Took the dog for a walk, cleaned the kitchen, and swept the floors. That may not seem like much, but it's not noon yet, and meds usually have me down for most of the morning. I pushed through, because I could hear my friend's voice in my head, "Go girl, you can do it!" That helps. It also is an immense help that she understands the illness because she has been through it herself - at least depression.

There really isn't an excuse in the world to not take care of you. At almost 45, I feel like living more than I ever thought I would. It's just a pain to push. However, cleaning this morning made my mood lift - because it was clean. Makes you feel better, as do a lot of friends and formal therapy.

It helps to get coping skills for pushing yourself. You just take five minutes at a time, write lists to cross off tasks, don't feel like everything has to be done in one day, and for goodness sakes, don't get down on YOU for not being able to do it all. Nobody can.

When I woke this morning, I wanted to disappear back in the sheets, but I'm looking forward to more writing, making a lovely dinner, and walking the dog again tonight. It's a start.

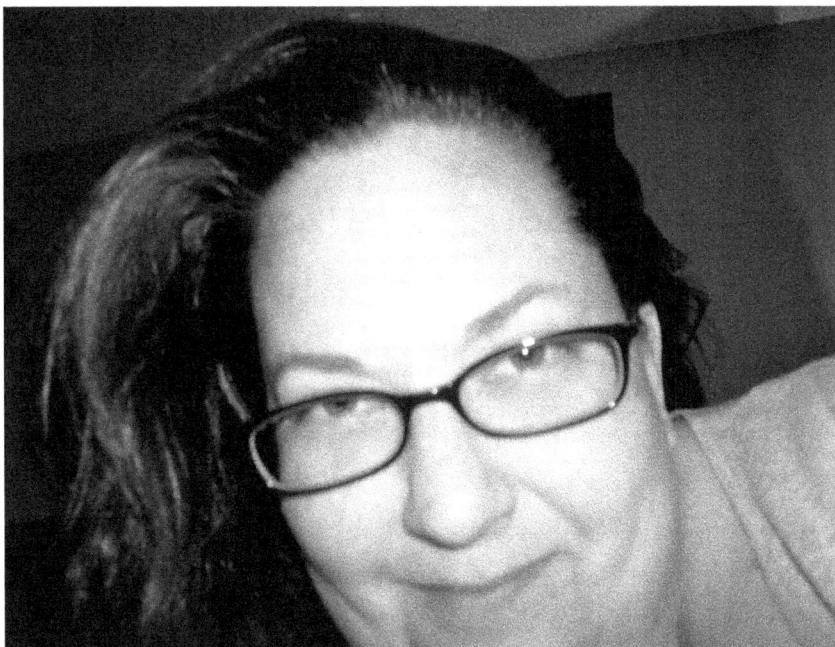

15

Unemployed #1 Excuse: You're Lazy

There are many myths to being unemployed, even more so for someone like me. After being a military wife and homemaker for many years, I found myself divorced and without an income. I immediately found part-time employment, then shortly after full-time.

I was laid off after a year.

It was all due to budget cuts, and with my specialties of teaching and writing, well - they lay more of us off every day. Here's what I've found in myself and the people I know that have been unemployed for part of the last five years:

Myths:

1. We're lazy. This is hysterical. There is no harder job than trying to find one. It's constant, stressful, and there's no security. Meanwhile, we have to improve our skills and pick up the slack around the house, while your mate works harder...

2. We don't want to work. HA! Who doesn't want to feel productive and make money? I know, there are some, but they are not the majority. Who wants to lose all they've worked for? No one.

3. We'd rather live off unemployment benefits. Love this one, particularly since I don't qualify for them. That's right, I spent too many years as a wife and mother, so I don't qualify for the benefits due to too few work credits. That goes for Medicaid as

well. No job, insurance, disability, or unemployment. This happens more than you know.

4. It's easy to get a job. Bullshit. There are so many of us in our forties and above that are having to settle for jobs outside our fields because of cuts, ageism, and too many new people with the magic potion of youth on their side. That's not bitter; it's a fact.

5. We limit ourselves. LOL I've looked overseas! I've not limited myself to any certain location, job type, or salary/hourly rate.

For me: my bipolar status, even if non-disclosed, makes it difficult to hold a steady job. However, labeled as high functioning - with my degrees, I should have one, right? After playing the "I'm employed/unemployed game," I decided to devote myself to writing. It's what I always wanted to do and went to college for.

For others: I've seen friends and family have to do everything from cleaning, telemarketing, being a server, and more to put food on the table. These are degreed people. They aren't lazy, they want more for themselves and their families, and they don't want a handout. They just want to work.

Happy.

16

Yoga=Mental Health

Yoga works. My journey with yoga started when my daughter was young, and we used to do it together on the carpet in the living room. We always felt great afterwards, so I decided to see if it was for me again. It is. The stretching, combined with a sweat-filled aerobic workout - just by holding poses - is awesome for your body. I'm pretty limber, as it runs in the family, and even though I'm a heavier chick, I can do most of the beginner stuff.

I went off a friend's suggestion and bought the yoga kit - mat, strap, and blocks, (Sports Authority - $32.00), and a DVD by Suzanne Deason from Barnes and Noble. The bookstore has a large yoga collection. I went for the 2 lb. hand weights as well, because I know my muscles need them. They hurt. However, the pain feels okay when I'm done, like I've accomplished something good for me.

How is it great for mental health? I am sleeping harder and longer, I'm calmer, and even though my body hurts from the movement, I'll get used to that.

The meditation portions of any given routine is essential for me to relax my mind. I hope to get good enough at it to be able to just relax anywhere, anytime. I have a cd of monks chanting, and that's great for the meditative part. I'm happier, even though my body is sore and still feels the illness and its shifts - my mind is more balanced.

Outside for exercise and light therapy.

17

Self-Therapies for Bipolar Patients

Living would be difficult without music! I'm truly, madly, and deeply in love with music. I've always used it to help care for my moods, but it wasn't until I interviewed a nurse practitioner about her use with music therapy in depressed and geriatric patients. I learned to use it effectively.

Now, I know that if I'm "up," that I need to play louder music, slowly lowering the volume and using different music until it is softer. "You meet the patient where they are, and then you adjust," claims Ruth McCaffrey, Professor at Florida Atlantic University. If I were depressed, I would start with slow music - even if it is depressing - and then move on to faster beats - and it brings me out of the blues.

Music=Life.

Light Therapy is another self-therapy that's very easy to do. Each morning, at the worst time of the day for your mood, go outside and sit in the sun for at least 10 minutes. The direct sunlight will feed you, and within the allotted time, you'll feel a lift in your mood. Indoor lighting does not count. Only natural light has the natural medicine you need.

Also, to combat insomnia, turn off the phone and the computer. Their backlighting mimics daylight, and it will keep you awake - the opposite of what you want. Unless it's an HD TV, you're okay on having the television on to sleep by. I need that.

Exercise! This is the most important one, yet the

hardest thing to motivate when you feel like a wet rag. Just a brisk walk out the door in your neighborhood, apartment parking lot, or a park somewhere will help motivate you for other activities in the day. "Move a muscle, change a thought," is one of the best pieces of advice I've had - because when I do it, it usually works.

For instance, I woke feeling horrible this morning, and I definitely was not going to write. I pushed to read my past blogs, and then I was ready to write another. It worked, and now I will feel like I've accomplished something instead of being lethargic and pitiful!

Exercise also helps depression in general. It gives me better sleep, I usually have a better appetite, and

I can move with ease. I'm just walking now, but I plan to put that to the test in the NAMI 5k walk in Orlando (Maitland). I think if I'm helping people, I'll be more motivated.

Switch off caffeine! This is an easy fix. Caffeine alters moods every day. The stimulation can make a bipolar patient more irritable, more hyper, and lead a person to self-medicate with a "downer," such as alcohol.

I drank for a long time when I was younger, as it helped "calm me." Now, I know that the alcohol only made me sadder, and actually hurt my sleeping and eating patterns. It also makes me even more hyper than usual, and that's no good. Anything that you feel switched your mood negatively, you should quit. It does make it easier to get along...

These main self-therapies are those that I use daily, particularly the music. Every day. It makes a tremendous difference, and it doesn't cost a fortune.

My graduation day with my daughter, Kristina.

18

Insomnia in Bipolar Patients

Tick Tock, Tick Tock goes the clock, while my husband snores gently. The snoring is not bad, but it irritates me that he can sleep and I'm wide-awake. Have I taken my meds? Of course. This is when the brain overrides the medication. There has been a lot of stress in my life lately, both good and bad, and I haven't had a good night's sleep more than one night in a row in over two months. I've tried everything: not turning on the computer, television, phone, or lights. All things are what my doctor suggested. They aren't working.

Chanting monks on CD make me zone and sleep. I almost missed a flight once due to them! However, music is irritating me now. It does when I'm like this. I'm anxious, worried, and exhausted. Maybe I'm too tired to sleep.

The problem is that if I don't sleep, I will go into mania. I don't want that, even though it really only means more sleepless nights. The best thing to sleep to if you have to have the TV on is, "Law and Order" on TNT, because it is a low noise show and darker in color. I may put that on. I think I'll write some more and check out the monks to put me to sleep tonight. Here's hoping it works...

A great day.

19

Bipolar and Happy Days!

Bipolar and "happy" don't usually go together like peas and carrots, but the combination does exist. Since I am a rapid-cycler, I can go from one mood to the next within minutes. Most do not. They will go through much longer periods of depression and then mania. Stability is what I seek, and it seems that it's here for a bit.

Since I went on new meds in December, they are finally getting themselves situated in my brain and being extremely effective. Yay! When my new hubby mentioned that my days are more even now, I was thrilled. Since I jump around in moods all day, it doesn't always seem like I'm stable - on the inside. I usually feel a bit of fear: of other people's reactions to me, seeming "different," and being tearful. But - I'm feeling productive and happy these days.

 I hope the change is for the better. Happy feels good; I enjoy other's company more, I want to go out often, and I love getting into projects. I'm crafty and welcome the relief of working with my hands for something other than writing. I think I'll take up pottery. Perhaps it could finance my writing career! Anyway, speaking of happy, I recently married for the second time.

I'll go back to being happy - taking advantage of a rare, extended stay of stability. :)

Kevin took this picture. A smile is always a good sign

ABOUT THE AUTHOR

Veronica Cronin received a Bachelor Arts degree in English from Florida Atlantic University and a Master of Arts degree in Creative Writing from Full Sail University. While writing into the wee hours of the night as a wife and mother, Veronica found success with the publications of her short story, "Bean Talk" in *Second Chicken Soup for a Woman's Soul*, her poetry, and her photography. She taught high school writing, writes as a columnist for *theexaminer.com*, and worked for The Walt Disney Company before writing her dramatic screenplay about a woman with bipolar illness, *All My By Self*, which earned her the Advanced Achievement Award in her graduate program. With her first publication, she's hoping some of the pixie dust from being a Fairy-Godmother-in-Training at the Magic Kingdom's castle hasn't worn off.

I

www.ingramcontent.com/pod-product-compliance
Lightning Source LLC
Chambersburg PA
CBHW050543280326
41933CB00011B/1702